YOUR SPACIOUS & SEASONAL YEAR

NOURISHING RITUALS, REFLECTIONS, AND RECIPES TO IGNITE JOY, CONNECTION, MEANING, AND MAGIC

ASHLEY BURNETT

Illustrated by Lela Shields

Copyright © 2023 by Ashley Burnett
Cover art and illustrations by Lela Shields

All rights reserved. No part of this publication may be reproduced, distributed, or transmitted in any form or by any means, including photocopying, recording, or other electronic or mechanical methods, without the prior written permission of the publisher, except in the case of brief quotations embodied in critical reviews and certain other noncommercial uses permitted by copyright law. For permission requests, write to the publisher addressed "Attention: Permissions Coordinator" at the address below.

This book is an educational and informational resource for anyone interested in spacious and seasonal living. I cannot guarantee the outcome of following the recommendations provided and my statements about the potential outcome are expressions of opinion only. I make no guarantees about the information and recommendations provided herein. By continuing to use/read/participate in this book, you acknowledge that I cannot guarantee any particular results, as such outcomes are based on subjective factors that are not within my control. Therefore, following any information or recommendations provided in this book is at your own risk. If you need medical advice, please hire a physician or other professional.

Ashley Burnett | Ashley Burnett & Co
info@ashleyburnett.co

Ordering Information:
Quantity sales. Special discounts are available on quantity purchases by corporations, associations, and others. For details, contact the "Special Sales Department" at the address above.

Your Spacious & Seasonal Year/ Ashley Burnett — 1st ed.
ISBN 979-8-218-32556-5

For my son Quintin…

may you remember to slow down,
connect with the earth, and
always remember
your magic.

CONTENTS

Foreword *by Monica Lucero*	9
Introduction	14
How to Use This Book	19
One: Winter Solstice	24
Two: Imbolc	32
Three: Spring Equinox	40
Four: Beltane	48
Five: Summer Solstice	56
Six: Lammas/Lughnasa	64
Seven: Fall Equinox	74
Eight: Samhain	82
Final Thoughts & Additional Resources	92
Acknowledgments	94
About the Author	96

Foreword

It is my great honor to preface Ashley's work as I have watched her create and refine these practices over the last 8 years. Working in harmony with the seasons is foundational to understanding our own cycles and rhythms and facilitates a deepening of our individual and collective wholeness. Ashley's curiosity, consistency, and contagious inspiration have touched the lives of many and will continue to do so! Her integration of seasonal self-inquiry, ritual, and herbalism makes for a dazzling transformational package.

Ashley has led by example, in showing us what a more spacious and feminine-focused leadership model looks like. It is not constantly burning the candle at both ends and simply pushing harder, but an acknowledgment that with spaciousness and tuning into nature's invitations, true and honest creativity is born.

I have witnessed her passion-based business thrive during a pandemic and the birth of her lively son! In pandemic years, we met outside for an entire year to do this work together through all seasons - even when a parka and gloves were necessary. This perseverance was sustaining on a soul level to a community of women during a time of connection-deprived isolation. And it was doing this work outside on the same piece of land for a full calendar year that really solidified the concepts.

Tuning our internal inquiries to the cycles of nature supports us in being present to what is, demonstrates the impermanence of it all, and inspires us to mirror the cyclical transformations of nature within ourselves with increased acceptance and grace. Furthermore, through this work, we can better choose how we interact with change and adversity - with more resilience, strength, and whole-self integration.

Ashley's check-ins allow us to write the stories of our lives from a lens of empowered positivity, a natural gift and way of life she embodies. Her work balances the shedding of past identities, honors the growing pains of life, acknowledges loss and grief, and features the important practice of celebration. She teaches us how to encourage the seedlings of potential we've had the courage to plant - and reminds us to appreciate all that we have created.

While this book focuses on self-inquiry, I will give you a magical suggestion: if you have a gift like Ashley does to consistently gather your favorite people in one physical or virtual space, please do (or recruit your friend who has that gift). It will multiply your understanding of these concepts - and accountability will strengthen your chances of fulfilling your intentions. You may discover an ally through a time of adversity, or an opportunity to combine strengths in accomplishing your desires together.

I grew up in a women's circle and have always known the infinite value of what I call "the disco ball magic mirror that is circle", but leading retreats with Ashley over the past 8 years featuring the conversations and inquiries outlined in this book has been essential and profound in my realization of a truly empowered adulthood. They keep me honest and grounded, yet expansive and free.

I have been blessed to witness a myriad of life's celebrations, losses, and identity/role/career shifts, bringing a greater capacity for compassion, acceptance, strength, and surrender to the constant evolutionary process of life. Through this work, I've found healing and closure from pieces of my past I had yet to examine and forgive, and gained wisdom and foresight of what is yet to come.

Consistent self-inquiry based on nature helps us discover our own true nature - the one that is wise, joyful, honest, and engaged. It is a practice to enliven this nature and reframe any perceived obstacles that get in our way... And whether you engage with this book alone or in community, please do not forget to extend the compassion you have for others to yourself.

Ashley will guide you to be more integral with your time, commitments, and boundaries, empowered to make these changes as you see fit and shed your skin to dissolve and create new identities for yourself as seasons change. You are a part of nature and its cycles of birth, death, and regeneration.

May this text inspire your steadfastness
towards your dreams and the discovery of a greater interconnectedness with life itself.

Blessings on the path.

May you grow to know:

the balance and harmony of your rhythms,

the grit and satisfaction of your labors,

that you can rest in the belly of Winter's darkness,

that your tears and sweat are indistinguishable when you learn to let go,

swim in the river,

and bring your whole self along.

~ Monica Lucero

"Live in each season as it passes; breathe the air, drink the drink, taste the fruit, and resign yourself to the influence of the earth."

~ Henry David Thoreau

Introduction

We're experiencing a ripe moment in history where so many of us are getting the intuitive nudge that it's time to *slow ourselves down*.

We're yearning for more space in our days for authentic connection with our loved ones. We're craving more room for self-care, rest, and treasured time off. We're desiring more direction, passion, and purpose in our lives. And we're longing for more meaning, magic, and soulful connection with ourselves, the natural world, and our extended communities.

It's no wonder we're feeling a sense of disconnection and unfulfillment given the fast-paced, tech-driven age that we're living in - let alone processing the aftermath of a multi-year isolating pandemic.

We've never been more digitally connected as a human collective - but have simultaneously never been more physically and emotionally isolated.

And it's taking its toll.

I believe that's why we're getting this nudge to operate our lives, workdays, and businesses in a different way. . .

In a way that NOURISHES versus depletes us, honors the wisdom of our ancestors, and allows us to lead our lives seasonally and sustainably - where we leave most days feeling satisfied, replenished, and fulfilled, rather than burned the eff out and frazzle-dazzled.

Something that's been most impactful for me in creating more spaciousness, satisfaction, meaning, and joy, in both my personal life - and in the daily flow of my business, has been to work more intentionally with the seasons, rhythms, and cycles of the natural world.

In 2016 I was introduced by one of my mentors, Joanna Lindenbaum, to something called the Wheel of the Year - an ancient annual cycle of seasonal festivals of the sun.

Many societies around the world have utilized working closely with their culture's version of these seasonal festivals and The Wheel, to honor and acknowledge the transition of the sun throughout the cycle of a year.

The seasonal celebrations occur evenly spaced eight times throughout the year and consist of the Winter Solstice, Spring Equinox, Summer Solstice, and Fall Equinox - and the direct halfway points in between them, signifying the coming season ahead.

Seasonal changes were very important to ancient societies - and still are to this day for many farming civilizations around the world that utilize the seasons to determine when to plow, sow, harvest, and rest.

In this book, we'll cycle along with the version of the seasonal festivals that I've been introduced to (and those of my ancestors... the ancient Celts), and I'll highlight the themes of each season and offer ideas for grounding rituals, recipes, and reflection questions for each.

When I started working more intentionally with the seasons in this way, the experience was SO profound for me...

I began to heal my body and soul on a deep cellular level. I began to honor my age and the phase of life that I found myself in. I began to experience less resistance to the darker months of the year. My business began to flow and flourish in ways I never thought possible. And I ended up weaving seasonality into every program that I offered my business coaching clients and women's circle participants.

I also started experiencing more joy, time freedom, meaning, and connection in my personal life, relationships and in my business. And I felt empowered, and most importantly, like MYSELF again.

This is my wish for you too – especially after navigating the particularly trying years of the pandemic.

What I want for you through reading this book, is to feel a deep sense of permission within your bones that it is totally OKAY, and necessary, to slow down and create space to replenish your reserves.

I want you to know that it's all right to set boundaries around your time, to turn off tech, to not answer that text right away, and to create sacred space for self-care, ritual, creativity, and rest.

I want you to remember that you are a part of nature, not separate from it – and that the natural world is longing for you to connect deeper with it... to cycle up energetically with its seasons, and to stop and smell the roses, often.

And my wish for you is that you feel deeply nourished and super inspired to ritualize working with the seasons in a more intentional way – resulting in more joy, connection, meaning, and magic!

How to use this book

WINTER SOLSTICE
December 21

SAMHAIN
November 1

IMBOLC
February 1

FALL EQUINOX
September 22

SPRING EQUINOX
March 20

LAMMAS
August 1

BELTANE
May 1

SUMMER SOLSTICE
June 21

Your Spacious & Seasonal Year is divided into 8 chapters highlighting the themes of each season in the Northern Hemisphere where I live (if you live in the Southern Hemisphere, just flip it!) and offers ideas for grounding rituals, recipes, and reflection questions for each.

You can feel free to read the book fully through initially if you feel inspired, and I also recommend looking at The Wheel icon above and marking each of the seasonal celebration dates on your calendar.

Note that while the in between seasonal dates are fixed, the Solstice and Equinox dates shift slightly per year, so for the most accurate date please check Google or your calendar on the day of or days surrounding each respective seasonal shift. On that day, I invite you to create some "blank space" in your day to turn off the TV, put your phone on silent mode, grab a cuppa tea and dive into that chapter of the book.

You could create a little mini-retreat for yourself to dive into all the seasonal suggestions over a 2 to 3-hour period.

You could commemorate each season with a 3-day seasonal kick-off plan - journaling one evening, building your seasonal altar the next morning, holding a simple ritual that night, then making the suggested recipe the following day.

Or, maybe you just rock out one of the seasonal suggestions that is most speaking to you in the moment… however you feel called to approach utilizing this book is all good!

A Little More on Seasonal Altars & Ritual

Each chapter of the book features seasonal ritual ideas including suggestions for building a seasonal altar. A seasonal altar is an energetic focal point and dedicated space for you to gather your dreams, wishes, and intentions for each season. It's also a sweet way to honor each seasonal shift and can act as a foundational reminder for your daily rituals to take place.

Creating your seasonal altar can be super simple. You can utilize items that you have on hand, or that you can access from mama nature herself. Each chapter will offer color and item suggestions – but feel free to add your own energy and flair!

As for where to build your seasonal altar? Anywhere! You can pop up an altar in your bedroom, on an end table or a dresser, on a mantle, or honestly, even on top of your printer like I often do! You can also set one up outdoors… think old stumps, on stones, or in hollow nooks of trees – just like that book, *Little Altars Everywhere*.

Also during this book, I frequently reference the word ritual.

To me ritual is an intentional act or action performed with reverence that can help us commemorate something, make something special, move through challenges, transitions, and hardships, and create more meaning, magic, and joy in our lives.

Ritual can be a one-off experience to honor and acknowledge big transitions or rite of passage moments (such as leaving a job, becoming a parent, going through menopause, or moving into a new home) or can be ritualized as a series of daily repeated actions that when done with intention can help us feel more connected with our sense of purpose, spirituality, inner worlds, and the natural world around us.

I don't go deep into how to craft specific rite of passage rituals in this book (I'm saving that for another book!), but I do offer ritual ideas for each season to help you feel more in tune with yourself and connected with each seasonal shift.

May this book serve you well and may it help you in creating your most spacious, joyful, and magical year yet!

*"What good is the warmth of summer, without
the cold of winter to give it sweetness."*

~ John Steinbeck

ONE

WINTER SOLSTICE
December 21st

Before working with the seasons, I always resisted winter... you too? Originally from the Midwest (I just migrated back after 18 years in Cali!), I dreaded the cold and constant dreary days.

But now I welcome the darkness... and the truth is that during this insular time of year, our human bodies and minds hold a deep need to hibernate, restore our reserves, and take in ample nourishment from mama earth – although many of our modern holiday traditions resist these actions.

The Winter Solstice marks the shortest day and longest night of the year. And while the darkness will still reign for a few more months, this day officially marks the coming of the light – as after today, the days will gradually grow longer in length.

By this point of the year most deciduous trees in the northern hemisphere have shed their leaves allowing them to expend less energy and take in more nutrients from the earth during this time.

Just like our tree allies, this is an optimal moment to nourish ourselves – but only if we give ourselves permission to slow down enough to reap the benefits.

This is also a potent time to reflect on the past year and to acknowledge all the transformations, blessings, and gifts that have been occurring in our lives – and it's a ripe moment for dreaming, visioning, and setting intentions for the coming year ahead.

Winter Reflection Questions

1. Reflect on what has come to fruition for you this year and ask yourself: What would I like to honor, own, and celebrate?

2. What are my top three "golden nuggets" from this year that I'd like to savor, and why?

3. What are some of the deepest lessons I've learned this year?

4. What am I calling in for myself in the coming year ahead — both on an "inner" personal growth level and "outer" production/goal level?

5. What energy would I like to lead with this coming season and year?

6. Considering what I'm calling in, what is my anchoring intention for the new year (a word or phrase to anchor my new year goals, visions, and dreams)?

Ritual Ideas & Creative Practices

Build a Winter Altar

- Find a special dedicated space for your altar creation.

- Start with a pretty scarf or piece of fabric as the base and build from there.

- Color Palette Suggestions: red, green, gold, white, silver.

- Altar Item Ideas: yule log, pinecones, evergreen sprigs, candles, bells, berries, and your dreams and intentions for the new year written on festive cards.

Fire Offering Ritual

- On a piece of paper, write down what you're ready to release from this year, stream of conscious style (fears/limiting beliefs/old habits/physical items).

- When you're complete, place cleansing winter herbs like pine, rosemary, or sage in the middle of the piece of paper, then wrap the herbs up with the paper, creating a little package.

- Meditate on what you're letting go of as you release the package safely into a hearth fire or fireplace.

- As the fire burns away what you're releasing, consider what will open up for you on the other side of that release.

Claim Your Intention for the Year

- Write your word or phrase of intention for the coming year (that you uncovered in the winter reflection questions) on something beautiful such as a wooden cut-out ornament, a little piece of paper that you slip into a glass ornament, or a large stone.

- Place it on your winter altar and meditate or journal on it throughout the season.

Featured Recipe

Wassail

The word 'wassail' comes from the Anglo-Saxon phrase 'waes hael' which means 'good health' in Old English. Folks would make wassail from ale, wine, or juice with warming spices such as clove, cinnamon, and star anise. It was drunk as part of the act of wassailing – an ancient ritual that included singing from door to door to spread wishes of good health and cheer and is where our modern version of caroling derived from.

There were also wassailing rituals performed in apple orchards – singing and thanking the trees for their production and promoting a good harvest for the coming year.

For the past 5 or so years, I've served wassail to my retreat and circle participants in the autumn and winter seasons, and it is such a hit as it's absolutely delicious and fills one's space with the most incredible aromas!

Ingredients:

- 8 cups organic apple cider or juice
- 2 apples
- 2 oranges
- 8 whole cloves
- 4 star anise pods
- 3 cinnamon sticks
- Lemon, honey, or fresh ginger to taste

Directions:

- Slice the oranges and apples crosswise into quarter-inch slices to reveal the 5-point star in the center of the apple and the pretty sections of the orange.
- Add the slices and all the ingredients to a large pot over medium-low heat.
- Bring to a gentle simmer and simmer for 30-45 minutes.
- Ladle into mugs and enjoy! (Feel free to strain if you'd like, but I love having an apple and orange slice in my mug.)

*"Let us nurture the spirit of renewal and embrace
the light of the lengthening days."*

~ Susan Gaylord

TWO

IMBOLC
February 1st

Having lived the past 18 years in the San Francisco Bay Area, the season of Imbolc was always an exciting time for me filled with the energy of promise and hope... the acacia tree in our yard started blooming its yellow pom-pom style flower clusters just as February hit, and some early spring herbs would begin to bud up out of the earth.

Now that I've moved back to my hometown in the Midwest, I'll have to be a little more patient as the cold, snow, and ice will halt the early spring budding that I've been used to – but I'll still begin noticing the days lengthening all the same.

The seasonal festival of Imbolc (meaning In the Belly in Gaelic) marks the exact midpoint between the Winter Solstice and the Spring Equinox. This is the time of year when Mama Earth is ripe with possibility, taking a moment of pause before launching into the fullness of spring.

This coming of spring season centers on the themes of new beginnings, fresh perspective, faith, hope, and trust – hope in a fruitful new growing season, and trust that our dreams and visions will come to fruition.

One of the rituals I most love prioritizing at this time of year is starting seeds for my spring garden – as well as figuratively planting seeds of intention for the coming season. Planting a new plant, building a spring altar, and writing down your intentions on little flower petals or seed packets are other fun ideas too.

This is also a sweet time for clearing out what's not working or serving you, as well as for some foundational planning for your upcoming spring projects.

Imbolc Reflection Questions

1. What literal or figurative seeds am I intending to plant this year?

2. When those seeds of intention blossom, what will that open up for me?

3. How can I infuse the theme of fresh perspective into this new year and upcoming season?

4. Where in my life would I benefit from weaving in a sense of pause and breath before spring is in full swing?

5. What am I ready to purify and let go of in my personal or professional life? What next right actions would I like to put into place?

Ritual Ideas & Creative Practices

Build an Imbolc Altar

- ✧ Find a special dedicated space for your altar creation.

- ✧ Start with a pretty scarf or piece of fabric as the base and build from there.

- ✧ Color Palette Suggestions: pale pink, yellow, moss green, white, lavender.

- ✧ Altar Item Ideas: flower buds, seeds, seed starts, small plants, fresh spring candles, amethyst crystals.

Start Seeds, or Plant a Small Plant

- ✧ As you start your seeds or plant your new plant, infuse your dreams, hopes, wishes, and prayers for the year into the soil.

- ✧ Water your seeds and intentions and put them in a warm sunny space for them to germinate, sprout, and grow.

- ✧ Lightly water your seeds, and continue to nurture and send them love, daily.

- ✧ If you planted a small plant, you could place it on your altar to remind yourself of your intentions.

Make Possibility Petals

- Cut out craft or construction paper in the shape of seeds or petals.

- Write your intentions on them and place them on your altar.

- You can also punch a small hole through them and tie them with string to a pretty branch.

- You could alternatively place your petals in a glass jar, plant them in the earth, mark your spot with a crystal or rock, and dig them up at the year's end to see what has come to fruition.

Featured Recipe

Soothing Herbal Bath Salts

One of my absolute favorite ways to ease tension or chill out after a long day is taking a luxurious bath with soothing salts. However, bath salts from the store can be pricey, and I don't know about you, but I will go through the entire jar in a week!

Making them at home is super simple and cost-effective, and they make great gifts too. You can switch the herbs up each season, but these are my favorites for the coming of spring.

Ingredients:

- 3 cups Epsom salts
- 1 cup coarse sea salt
- 2 tablespoons almond, olive, or apricot kernel oil
- 3 tablespoons dried flowers or herbs such as sage, lavender, and rose
- 7 drops lavender, 7 drops chamomile, and 7 drops sage essential oils (or the essential oils of your choice)

Directions:

- With clean hands, mix all ingredients in a large glass bowl, infusing your wishes and prayers for the coming season as you mix.
- Store in a cool dry place in an airtight container or mason jar until the next use (up to 3 months).
- Scoop ½ to 1 cup of the mixture into your bath, and soak in the healing magic.

"It's a spring fever. That is what the name of it is. And when you've got it, you want to—oh, you don't quite know what it is you do want, but it just fairly makes your heart ache,
you want it so!"

~ Mark Twain

THREE

SPRING EQUINOX
March 20th

Spring is most definitely my favorite season of the year… The energy of freshness and possibility abound — and this Aries has gotta shout it out from the rooftops that it's her birth season too!

The Spring Equinox kicks off the launch into the brighter months of the year and is a welcome reprieve from the dark and dreary months prior. On the auspicious day of the Spring Equinox, light and dark are at a place of equilibrium and balance - and from this point forward, the light begins to override the dark.

Spring is a season of renewal, cleansing, blossoming, and igniting our sense of playfulness, pleasure, and joy. It's an ideal time for clearing out what doesn't serve - both on an inner and outer level, such as embarking on spring cleaning or organizational projects, or a digital detox or juice cleanse.

It's also a ripe moment for embarking on creative projects as we're finally emerging out of our cozy winter nests and getting those hits of inspiration to make or create.

Spring Reflection Questions

1. What areas of my life would benefit from some spring cleaning? (business, relationships, wellness, etc.)

2. How specifically would I like to cleanse these areas out?

3. How can I infuse the themes of fresh energy and perspective into what I'm cleansing or clearing?

4. How will my life positively shift after the cleansing is completed? What's on the other side of that clearing process?

5. How will I act and feel differently once these areas are cleared out?

6. What's my next right action to take?

Ritual Ideas & Creative Practices

Build a Spring Altar

- Find a special, dedicated space for your altar creation.
- Start with a pretty scarf or piece of fabric as the base and build from there.
- Color Palette Suggestions: Light yellow, seafoam green, periwinkle, pink, and other pastel colors.
- Altar Item Ideas: Decorated eggs, aquamarine crystals, beeswax candles, spring flowers, fertility symbols, words associated with pleasure, confidence, and renewal.

Make a Spring Flower Crown

Supplies:

- 1 roll of floral tape
- 2 feet of wired hemp or paper-covered wire (I like 18 gauge by Ashland)
- A large, trimmed bouquet of flowers and herbs of your choice
- Wire cutters and scissors

Instructions:

- Wrap the wired hemp around your head to determine the diameter of your crown, then twist the ends around each other to fasten - taking care to bend the ends flush to the crown.

- Make small bouquets of flowers (3-6 stems each), trimming the stems to 2-3 inches in length.

- Take your mini bouquet and wrap floral tape around it until it's secure - stretching the tape slightly so that it can adhere to itself.

- Place your mini bouquet next to the wired hemp crown and wrap the two together with floral tape.

- You can rock a super minimal 1920s style crown, featuring just one flower bouquet, and wearing it to one side of your head (super fun!), or you can make a full crown by making multiple bouquets, facing them all in the same direction, and placing and wrapping them staggered, one over the next.
  (8 or so bouquets would make a full crown, but I find that too much work and I love making them super minimal!)

- Be sure to snap a pic of yourself in your crown and tag me on IG at @ashleyburnettco - I would love to see it!

Take a Spring Herbal Walk

If you're familiar with the herbs in your area, spring is the perfect season to say hello to them by taking a slow and grounding herbal walk on the land you live on, or at a park nearby.

If you're unfamiliar with the herbs and plants in your area, this is an ideal time to hire an herbalist to take you on a local herbal walk. On the walk, they'll point out common medicinal and edible spring herbs, and will potentially show you how to harvest, process, and make herbal medicines with them.

If you're familiar with which herbs are edible in your area, this season can be a beautiful time to start harvesting if they're in abundance. I like to ask permission from the plant first for it to be picked and pick just the amount that you'll use for cooking or medicine making. You can also practice reciprocity with the plant by singing to it as you harvest – one of my favorite ways to harvest herbs and flowers! (P.S. Please make sure that you're 100% sure of each plant's ID before working with them.)

Featured Recipe

Nourishing Spring-Cleaning Tea Blend

Making an herbal tea blend is simple and fun, and home-blended teas are exceptional compared to the bagged teas most of us are used to drinking.

You can either use dried herbs that you've grown yourself in your garden, herbs that grow wild in abundance in your area, or herbs that you order from a store in bulk (I love Mountain Rose Herbs).

This is my take on a spring-cleaning detox tea - which is also calming and soothing to the nervous system as the busy-bee spring energy kicks into gear.

Ingredients:

- 1 cup dried nettles
- 1 cup dried thyme leaves
- 1 cup dried red clover
- ¼ cup dried calendula petals

Directions:

- Combine all the dried herbs together in an airtight container or mason jar, stir to evenly distribute the plant material, and store it for future use (this recipe should nearly fill up a quart-sized jar).
- Use 1 tablespoon of the tea blend per cup of boiling water.
- Steep covered in your teapot or vessel of choice for 10-30 minutes, to capture all the medicinal volatile oils in the plant matter… don't let them steam away!
- Add a spoonful of honey and a splash of cow's or nut milk if desired.
- Take a deep breath in, and a deep breath out, and enjoy your bliss.

*P.S. This tea can be made using fresh herbs as well, but please use caution and wear gloves while handling fresh nettles as they can sting!

"Come with me into the woods. Where spring is advancing, as it does, no matter what, not being singular or particular, but one of the forever gifts, and certainly visible."

~ Mary Oliver

FOUR

BELTANE
May 1st

On the beautifully wild Petaluma, CA based property that I lived on and led my women's circles and business retreats at for the past 8 years, the wild tom turkeys frequently fanned their tail feathers during the season of Beltane, always on the lookout for a mate.

Many a morning I'd be woken up at 4 or 5 am by their awkward "gobble-gobble" call - trying their damnedest to woo a sweet hen… and once I even caught two turkeys in the act!

The seasonal festival of Beltane (meaning Bright Fire in Gaelic), marks the exact midpoint between the Spring Equinox and the Summer Solstice and honors the earth's fertility and creative energy.

This season celebrates the fullness of spring, welcomes the coming heat and light of summer, and centers the themes of sensuality, sexuality, pleasure, creativity, and passion.

Beltane celebrates our aliveness and creative expression. This season is all about following your heart and doing what feels most pleasurable to you.

I also find that my creative energy is heightened during this time and is often when I get big hits of inspiration and my best business ideas come through. If you're an entrepreneur, or you work frequently on creative side projects, this is a ripe time for starting them or seeing them through to fruition.

Beltane Reflection Questions

1. What brings me joy?

2. What ignites a sense of pleasure in my life?

3. If I were to up my pleasure and joy game, what would my day/week/month/year look like?

4. What do I need to say yes to, and no to in order to prioritize what brings me joy and pleasure?

5. What do I feel will positively shift for me in my life when I prioritize these things?

6. What might open up or become possible for me from that place?

Ritual Ideas & Creative Practices

Build a Beltane Altar

- ⟡ Find a special, dedicated space for your altar creation.

- ⟡ Start with a pretty scarf or piece of fabric as the base and build from there.

- ⟡ Color Palette Suggestions: bright pinks, reds, purples, and vibrant spring colors.

- ⟡ Altar Item Ideas: blossoming flowers, fertility symbols, candles, rose water, and words associated with pleasure and joy.

Flowering Foot Bath Ritual

- ⟡ Gather fresh blossoms and herbs from around your property or nearby (rose, lavender, mint, and calendula are some of my favorites).

- ⟡ Fill a large bowl or basin with warm water.

- ⟡ Add in ¼ cup Epsom salts, 3-4 drops of essential oils (rose and lavender are great options), the fresh flowers, and your intentions for the Beltane season.

- ⟡ Find a comfortable and cozy place to sit (either indoors or outdoors) and place your feet gently in the nourishing foot bath.

- Close your eyes, take a few deep grounding breaths, and let the healing bath work its magic for 10-15 minutes - soaking in your intentions for the season.

- Towel dry and enjoy your relaxed bliss.

Intentional Outdoor Tea Party

- Invite a few of your besties over for a late afternoon or early evening outdoor tea party.

- Steep your favorite flowering herbal tea blend (check out the featured recipe in the previous chapter!) in a pretty teapot for 10-30 minutes.

- Serve in dainty teacups, along with your favorite healthy sweet treats.

- As you're sipping the tea, ask each of your guests to share their intentions for the summer months ahead, and what they're currently celebrating and grateful for.

- Offer a bit of the tea to Mama Earth, offering blessings and thank yous to the land you reside on.

- Compost the spent herbs to the earth after you're finished with your party.

Featured Recipe

Rose Infused Honey

7 years ago, I completed an herbal medicine training program at the California School of Herbal Studies in Forestville, CA, founded by well-known herbalist Rosemary Gladstar. I'd been fascinated by our medicinal plant allies for years and was so grateful to receive training at such a stunning and revered place.

One of the most simple and delicious practices I learned was how to make herbal-infused honey, and one of my favorite plants to infuse into my honey is rose... so delish! May this recipe open your heart, ignite your passion, and inspire your creative soul!

Ingredients:

- Dried, unsprayed, organic or wild rose petals (I love using the French 'Cécile Brünner' rose for this)
- Raw, local honey

Directions:

- Fill a clean pint or quart jar (depending on how much infused honey you'd like to make) about ⅓ of the way full with the dried roses.
- Pour your honey into the jar over the plant matter and be sure that your herbs are fully submerged.
- Place a lid on the jar and keep it in a warm and sunny spot, turning the jar over a few times once per day.
- Infuse for 1-3 weeks, then strain and enjoy on muffins, bread, in tea, or just by the spoonful. Store in a cool, dark place.
- You can also make this recipe with fresh rose petals (which I love doing) but please note that your honey will be runny from the water in the plant material. I also prefer to store fresh infused honey in the fridge to help maintain freshness.

"Summer is the annual permission slip to be lazy. To do nothing and have it count for something. To lie in the grass and count the stars. To sit on a branch and study the clouds."

~ Regina Brett

FIVE

SUMMER SOLSTICE
June 21ˢᵗ

Ahhhh summer... the season of fun, play, warmth, and vacations. Those hot summer nights are beckoning us to stay up late and soak in their fun-loving magic, and the draw to "check out" of our daily routine is strong.

The Summer Solstice marks the longest day and shortest night of the year – yet from this moment forward, the days will indeed begin to shorten.

This enchanting season honors the light within each of us and is a powerful time to connect to what lights us up and makes us feel most playful, radiant, and fully self-expressed.

As I mentioned before, the desire to check out during this time of year is strong. I believe this is partially due to the Summer Solstice landing opposite of the Winter Solstice on the Wheel, and oftentimes dichotomies feature similarities.

This is why I build in a month-long seasonal sabbatical during the month of July – completing my spring programming and signing off from running the daily operations of my business, as well as from email and social media during this time.

Summer Reflection Questions

1. What lights me up and makes me feel playful and like the most radiant version of myself?

2. What actions and activities that I engage in make me feel this way?

3. In what areas of my life do I need a playfulness and radiance boost?

4. How can I weave some of that energy (what makes me feel most playful and radiant) into the areas that need a boost?

5. What am I claiming and committing to this summer and for the second half of this year?

6. What are my next right-aligned actions or rituals to take?

Ritual Ideas & Creative Practices

Build a Summer Altar

- ⟡ Find a special, dedicated space for your altar creation.

- ⟡ Start with a pretty scarf or piece of fabric as the base and build from there.

- ⟡ Color Palette Suggestions: yellows, oranges, white, and gold.

- ⟡ Altar Item Ideas: sun catchers, beeswax candles, sun symbols, and summer flowers such as sunflowers, craspedia, and black-eyed susan.

Create a Summer-Themed Outdoor Nature Altar

- ⟡ Go on a "Scavenger Hunt" foraging for natural items in your area. Collect stones, rocks, flowers, berries, leaves, bark, seeds, etc. Practice reciprocity by singing or offering a blessing to the earth as you gather your items.

- ⟡ With your finds, create a circular sun-inspired pattern around a center focal point (a candle, large crystal, or stone) contemplating your intentions for summer as you create.

- ⟡ Once completed, sit with the altar for 5-10 minutes and meditate on your intentions, wishes, and prayers for the season - and the second half of the year.

- ⟡ Blow out the candle (if you used one) and dissolve the altar at the end of the ritual - or feel free to continue to add to it over the next few days.

* This is also a fun activity to do with kiddos, family, and friends. If engaging in it with others, you can assign specific items for the "scavengers" to go find, then build your sun-inspired summer altar together.

Barefoot Outdoor Walking Meditation Practice

- Find an outdoor natural environment that feels calming to practice in.

- Remove your shoes and plant your feet firmly on the earth.

- Slowly and mindfully walk in one direction for 10-15 paces, taking deep and grounding breaths as you walk.

- Pause, take a deep breath, and fully take in your surroundings - then turn to a different direction, and repeat.

- Practice for 5-15 minutes and notice the sense of calm you feel afterward.

Featured Recipe

Summer Slumber Tea Blend

Making herbal tea is simple and fun, and home-blended teas are exceptional compared to the bagged teas most of us are used to drinking.

You can either use dried herbs that you've grown in your garden, that grow wild in abundance in your area, or herbs that you order from a store in bulk (I love Mountain Rose Herbs).

This is my take on a sleepytime tea blend, to help you calm down and replenish your reserves during those long summer nights.

Ingredients:

- 1 cup dried chamomile flowers
- 1 cup dried lemon balm leaves
- 1 cup dried milky oat tops
- ¼ cup dried lavender petals

Directions:

- Combine all the dried herbs together in an airtight container or mason jar, stir to evenly distribute the plant material, and store for future use (this recipe should nearly fill up a quart-sized jar).
- Use 1 tablespoon of the tea blend per cup of boiling water.
- Steep the blend covered in your teapot or vessel for 10-30 minutes to capture all the medicinal volatile oils in the plant matter… don't let them steam away!
- Add a spoonful of honey and a splash of cow's or nut milk if desired.
- Take a deep breath in, and a deep breath out, and enjoy your bliss.

*P.S. This tea can be made using fresh herbs as well.

"There is something so special in the early leaves drifting from the trees - as if we are all to be allowed a chance to peel, to refresh, to start again."

~ Ruth Ahmed

SIX

LAMMAS/LUGHNASA
August 1st

This in-between season holds a special place in my heart as I went into labor with my son Quintin on August 5th a little over 4 years ago. It was such a reflection of the season – of stripping away any additional noise or energy around me so that I could get uber-focused on the task at hand of birthing my sweet boy and caring for him, without distractions.

Lammas (meaning Loaf Mass in Old English) or Lughnasa (meaning the month of August in Gaelic) is the direct halfway point between the Summer Solstice and Fall Equinox. This is the spoke in the Wheel that signifies the first phase of the harvest season and is when we begin noticing the days growing shorter and the light of summer beginning to wane.

That said, this season can bring up some resistance to change – to shorter days, summer coming to a close, school starting, etc. As we all know, change can feel uncomfortable so mild feelings of edginess at this time of year are completely normal.

However, as I mentioned earlier, this is indeed a powerful moment to pause, reassess, and take stock of how our year has been unfolding, and to reignite the intentions we set at the start of the year before fall's hustle and bustle energy hits with full force.

This is about getting real to see what's working in our lives and what's not and stripping away what's not serving us toward reaching the visions we set for ourselves at the start of the year.

Lammas Reflection Questions

1. Call to mind the intentions that you set for yourself at the beginning of this year and ask yourself: Are my actions on track for bringing that vision to fruition?

2. What structures, habits, and activities need to be stripped away or shaken off in order to get fully on track with my vision

3. What am I holding onto that needs to be laid down so that I can align the trajectory of my goals for the remainder of this year?

4. How can I begin to release and shed the things that need releasing?

5. From this space of release, what am I declaring to say yes to and step into for the remainder of this year?

6. What is my next right action to take?

Ritual Ideas & Creative Practices

Build a Lammas Altar

- ✧ Find a special, dedicated space for your altar creation.

- ✧ Start with a pretty scarf or piece of fabric as the base and build from there.

- ✧ Color Palette Suggestions: oranges, browns, yellows, straw, and umber.

- ✧ Altar Item Ideas: grains, dried corn, straws, seed pods, candles, remainder-of-year intentions, crystals or stones in harvest colors, yellow flowers, or dried leaves.

Self-Massage Practice

- ✧ Directly after bathing or showering, lay a large towel on the ground and sit on it with your legs lengthened.

- ✧ With your favorite massage oil or infused oil (see recipe to follow) massage your limbs with long and slow strokes.

- ✧ Take care to stop at some of the "crunchy" places and spend more focused time massaging there (your feet, shoulders, lower back, and forearms).

- As you're massaging yourself, contemplate what you're releasing or shedding, and what you're calling in for the remainder of the year.

- When you feel complete, lay down on your back with your knees bent, feet on the floor, with one hand on your heart and the other on your belly, and send your body gratitude for all that it does for you on a daily basis.

- Towel the oil off gently and sleep well!

Create a Spacious & Sustainable Fall Schedule

One of my favorite practices that I guide my entrepreneurial coaching clients through, and that I prioritize quarterly in my business, is to create a spacious and sustainable, seasonal schedule that is easy to manage – versus jam-packed with endless to-do's.

In this practice, I help my clients:

- ✧ Set strong boundaries around the time they're working on and in their business for each season, and when they're not.

- ✧ Clarify their non-negotiable self-care, creativity, and joy blocks.

- ✧ Determine their longer and shorter seasonal breaks and sabbaticals.

- ✧ Discover updated ways to scale their businesses that also leverage their free time.

This practice has benefited even my non-entrepreneur clients and circle members, supporting them in setting stronger boundaries around their time and reclaiming hours of space to spend more time with their loved ones.

If this is speaking to you, I invite you to type the following link in your browser to sign up to receive the recording of my *Reclaim Your Time Freedom Workshop* and get ready to let the good times roll.

https://ashleyburnett.co/seasonalschedule

Featured Recipe

Detoxifying Herbal Massage Oil

Ingredients:

- ✧ 1 cup calendula petals
- ✧ 1 cup rose petals
- ✧ 1 cup lavender flowers
- ✧ Organic extra light olive oil
- ✧ Optional: 20 drops of lavender essential oil

Directions:

- Place herbs in a crock pot or double boiler, and fully cover with organic extra-light olive oil (or another carrier oil of choice), leaving at least an inch or two of oil above the herbs.

- Gently heat the herbs over very low heat (preferably between 100° and 140° F for about an hour or so) until the oil takes on the scent of the herbs.

- Once the oil is cooled, strain using a cheesecloth, nut milk bag, or fine mesh strainer.

- Add in the drops of lavender oil if desired.

- Bottle and label in dry, sterilized glass bottles, and store in a cool, dark, dry place for up to six months.

"No spring nor summer beauty hath such grace as I have seen in one autumnal face."

~ John Donne

SEVEN

FALL EQUINOX
September 22nd

I adore fall... drinking fresh pressed apple cider, pear and apple processing, and pumpkin bread making are some of my most cherished autumn memories.

The Fall Equinox is one of two auspicious days out of the year where day and night are in equal balance and is a season of gratitude and celebration. This exuberant time of year celebrates the fullness of harvest season – and honors our unique brilliance as individuals, as well as the celebratory energy of fall.

This is a sweet moment to applaud our hard work and to acknowledge all the ways we've been showing up in the world. It's also a time to give gratitude for our own personal harvests, and to literally and figuratively reap the fruits of our labor – even if what has manifested thus far isn't exactly what we thought it would look like!

This season also signifies the imminent inward turn and is a time of planning and preparation for the cold and dark months that lie ahead.

Autumn Reflection Questions

1. What am I currently harvesting and celebrating this fall?

2. What have I accomplished this year (or am I on track to achieve) that I'd like to recognize?

3. What gifts have I received this year so far? Write down even unexpected gifts, challenges, and lessons that perhaps have been blessings in disguise.

4. In terms of my harvest, what am I grateful for, and what's been working?

5. What needs shifting or updating to more deeply align with my dreams and vision?

6. What's something that hasn't yet come to fruition that I'd like to call in for the remainder of this year, and what's one next right action or ritual to help me get there?

Ritual Ideas & Creative Practices

Build an Autumn Altar

- ✧ Find a special, dedicated space for your altar creation.

- ✧ Start with a pretty scarf or piece of fabric as the base and build from there.

- ✧ Color Palette Suggestions: reds, golds, oranges, browns, or other autumnal shades.

- ✧ Altar Item Ideas: corn, pumpkins, autumn leaves, apples, seed pods, shelled nuts, crop and harvest symbols.

Autumnal Leaf & Flower Ritual

- ✧ Find your favorite flower field, farm, or garden, and take a 20-minute silent meditation walk while creating a bouquet to reflect your own personal expression (a unique reflection of you)

- ✧ As you're gathering your blooms, practice reciprocity with the Earth by singing a song or offering a wish of gratitude as a thank you as you pick.

- ✧ Share what your bouquet represents to you with a loved one, or better yet, take them with you to share the experience together.

Create a Gratitude Tree

- Cut out fall-themed paper or autumnal card stock in the shape of leaves and write words of gratitude on the leaves.

- Use a hole punch to create a hole and tie a pretty ribbon through it.

- Hang your leaves on trees outside your home or inside the home on a stick or branch, making a piece of meaningful and decorative art – and hang perhaps right above your fall altar so that you can meditate on them daily.

Featured Recipe

Homemade Cinnamon-Spiced Applesauce

When I was growing up, my mom and I would make homemade applesauce together every autumn, and I SO looked forward to smelling the warm and inviting scents of cinnamon and apples cooking down on the stove. We pretty much would wing it every time, but here's my take on her simple and easy sauce... thanks, Mom!

Ingredients:

- 12 cups organic apples, cored, and roughly peeled and sliced
- ½ cup water or apple juice
- Juice of ½ lemon
- 1/4 cup raw honey
- 1 tsp cinnamon or pumpkin pie spice – or more to taste

Directions:

- In a large pot, combine all ingredients and cook over medium heat for 30 to 40 minutes.
- Stir the mixture occasionally – and if it's getting too thick (depending on the juiciness of your apples) feel free to thin out slightly with a splash of water or apple juice.
- Once cooked through, let cool on the stove completely.
- Puree with a stick blender, blender, or food processor to the desired consistency.
- Store in the fridge in mason jars for up to a week or freeze for up to 3 months.

"Descent into the dark is an inevitable and necessary part of the cycle. To resist the times and lessons of the darkness is to be in resistance to the whole cycle because the whole cannot function without this part."

~ Jane Meredith

EIGHT

SAMHAIN
October 31st & November 1st

Located halfway in between the Fall Equinox and Winter Solstice - and roughly around the same calendar dates as Halloween, Day of the Dead, and All Saint's Day, Samhain (pronounced Sow-in, and meaning Summer's End in Gaelic) marks the end of the harvest season and launches the descent into the darkest months of the year.

During this mystical season, the spirit and magic realms are thin – allowing us to connect more deeply with our ancestors and the magic and mystery all around us.

While there's oftentimes resistance to this spoke of the year's cycle – death, closure, release, and shifting into hibernation mode creates the restoration needed to cultivate new beginnings and a new cycle ahead.

That said, this in-between season is an ideal time to take a good look at what projects need to be "tucked in" or completed before the year's end and to get prepared for the upcoming restorative winter months.

One of the rituals I most love doing during this season is to create my personal "Self-Care Hibernation Toolkit" (see ritual suggestion to follow).

This is all about creating a warm, cozy, magical, and super supportive indoor environment that invites deep rest and personal connection during the winter months (inspired by the Danish concept Hygge).

I also love setting boundaries around what time I shut off screens and lights at night, as well as setting stronger boundaries in my business around when I'm completing work for the day.

This is also a ripe time to get prepped for your winter breaks and sabbaticals, and to clarify what boundaries and support systems need to be put in place during those breaks (such as setting email auto responders, temporarily removing yourself from group text threads, social media detoxes, etc.) so that you can really "go dark" and fully reap the benefits of the inward turn.

This season holds so much potential for healing and nourishment for each of us – and if we allow ourselves to slow down and receive the gifts of the season, we'll be provided with the sustenance necessary to birth a fresh cycle with strength, vitality, and ground.

Samhain Reflection Questions

1. How would I like to feel during this sacred season of hibernation and restoration?

2. What will I do to prepare myself (both on an "inner" personal growth level and "outer" production level) to fully reap the benefits of the inward turn?

3. How much time would I like to take off during the holiday/winter season, and what projects need to be completed and "tucked in" to do so?

4. What boundaries and support pieces need to be put in place for me to take this time off and receive the restoration I'm seeking during the dark months ahead?

5. If I were to honor these intentions, what would positively shift for me, and what would be possible for me at the beginning of the upcoming year?

6. What actions and rituals will I devote myself to during this season of darkness?

Ritual Ideas & Creative Practices

Build a Samhain Altar

- ⟡ Find a special, dedicated space for your altar creation.

- ⟡ Start with a pretty scarf or piece of fabric as the base and build from there.

- ⟡ Color Palette Suggestions: rich oranges, golds, browns, or other autumnal shades.

- ⟡ Altar Item Ideas: pumpkins, fall leaves, Day of the Dead or Halloween items, photos of loved ones or ancestors who've passed, oracle decks, candles, crystals, seed pods, acorns, and any symbols of hibernation.

Create Your Self-Care Hibernation Toolkit

- ⟡ Gather or purchase items that create a warm, cozy, and magical indoor environment that invite deep rest and personal connection.

- ⟡ Examples of what to add to your toolkit: Candles, olde tyme lanterns, and candle holders (that you can use instead of electric lights), warm twinkle lights, cozy blankets, seasonal books and magazines, journals, bath salts, herbal tea blends, essential oils, meditation cushions, cozy sweaters and shawls, wool socks, food items for stews, soups, and stocks.

- Deck out the various rooms and spaces of your home (potentially even your work desk) with these items to help inspire a deep sense of comfort and joy.

Create An Outdoor Ancestor Offering

- Gather any biodegradable items that remind you of your ancestors that you'd like to present to them as an offering.

- Go to a special space in nature with your items and bring a photo of your ancestor with you.

- When you arrive at your special space, create an outdoor altar for them in their honor.

- Take your time creating it, and once you're complete, sit and meditate in front of the altar reflecting on who they were, the lessons you've learned from them, and the gifts you've received from them.

- When you've completed your meditation, you can either leave the altar there for a few days and bring a new item each day as a gift, or you can dissolve the altar.

Featured Recipe

Gluten-Free Chocolate Chip Pumpkin Bread or Muffins

Dry Ingredients:

- ✧ 1 cup all-purpose 1:1 gluten-free flour blend (you can also use wheat or all-purpose flour for this recipe)
- ✧ ¾ cup almond meal
- ✧ ¼ teaspoon baking powder
- ✧ 1 teaspoon baking soda
- ✧ 1 teaspoon salt
- ✧ 1 teaspoon cinnamon
- ✧ 1 teaspoon pumpkin pie spice

Additional Ingredients:

- 1 cup evaporated cane juice or coconut palm sugar
- ⅓ cup coconut oil, avocado oil, or butter
- 2 organic eggs
- 1 cup homemade pumpkin puree, or canned pumpkin
- ⅓ cup organic milk or almond milk
- ½ teaspoon vanilla extract
- ⅓ cup chocolate chips
- ⅓ cup chopped nuts
- ⅓ cup chopped dates, or organic raisins

Directions:

- Preheat the oven to 350° degrees.
- In a small saucepan, melt the coconut oil over low heat. Set aside.
- In a medium-sized bowl, sift together dry ingredients until well combined. Set aside.
- In a large bowl, whisk together sugar, oil, and eggs until light and fluffy.

- Whisk the pumpkin into the large bowl until well combined.

- In a glass measuring cup combine the milk and vanilla. Set aside.

- Add half of the dry ingredients to the pumpkin mixture and mix well with a large spoon or spatula – then add half of the milk, and fully combine. Repeat with the remaining dry ingredients and milk mixture.

- Stir in the chocolate chips, nuts, and raisins or dates.

- Pour batter into a buttered or oiled loaf pan, or lined muffin tin.

- For bread, bake for about 1 hour, or until bread is fully baked through. For muffins, bake for about 25 minutes, or until the muffins test done.

FINAL THOUGHTS & ADDITIONAL RESOURCES

Working intentionally with the seasonal shifts and rituals is a lifelong path and something that you can revisit and refine again and again, each year.

For me, it's taken regular seasonal check-ins and calendaring to maintain a deep connection with the seasons – hence why I recommend plugging the Wheel of the Year dates into your calendar upfront… but with time, living a life aligned with the seasons will start to feel like second nature.

If you'd like to take this work to the next level here are some additional next steps to take:

- ✧ Join our Ashley Burnett & CO newsletter list for continued seasonal inspo and to be looped in on our upcoming events and retreats.
  www.ashleyburnett.co

- ✧ Sign up for the Reclaim Your Time Freedom Workshop to clarify your aligned seasonal schedule and create more spaciousness and joy in your daily life.
  www.ashleyburnett.co/seasonalschedule

- ✧ Restore your reserves with an upcoming seasonal Replenish Retreat. Take a half-day time out to unwind, recalibrate your nervous system, be supported, and reflect on your visions and intentions for the season.
www.ashleyburnett.co/replenish

- ✧ For Entrepreneurs & Creatives: Uplevel your business with the Unleash Your Impact Online Training Course to make a more impactful positive ripple effect and expand your revenue through the advanced facilitation of group programs, women's circles & retreats.
www.ashleyburnett.co/unleash

Acknowledgments

I am beyond grateful for the opportunity to write this book and for all the support that has gone into making this long-term dream a reality. I would especially like to thank Joanna Lindenbaum, my business coach for 2 years who also trained me in ritual work and introduced me to the Wheel of the Year. Monica Lucero (aka Moni), one of my dearest friends and our ABC in-person Retreat Assistant for the past 8 years and Resident Coach for the past 2.5 – thank you for all the support throughout the years and for helping me to conceptualize many of the journaling questions and rituals for the yearlong seasonally focused women's circle, the Soulstice Sisterhood, of which a number of the reflection questions and ritual ideas for this book were inspired by. Amy D. Marie, my ABC Online Business Manager for 3.5 years turned Company Strategist and Resident Coach for the past 2.5, and the co-designer of this book – I literally could not have done this without you. Rani MacNeal – my ABC Community Care Maven and Virtual Assistant, as well as the co-designer and proofreader for this book – thanks for wearing all the hats and supporting this business for the past 8+ years – I couldn't have done this without your support either. And Lela Shields for your incredible artwork and illustration magic!

To our past ABC team members, thanks for helping to support the trajectory of this business over the years, and to all our ABC circle, retreat, and program participants past and present… your spirit has been contagious, and it's been an honor to collaborate with you and support you over the years.

Thank you to the Tiny Book Course team at Get It Done for helping me to take my content and flush it out into book format. Nancy Hopkins, Linda Finocchiaro, Erin Knapheide, and Robb & Jessica Connor for your generous support. Rosemary Gladstar and The California School of Herbal Studies for inspiring in me a deeper love and knowledge of plants. The women's circles, singing circles, training programs, and retreats that I've participated in that have helped shape my work and who I am today. My dearest friends, thank you for listening to me, playing with me, inspiring me, and guiding me.

My deepest gratitude to my supportive husband David Kucera for believing in me and making bold moves alongside me. For the light of my life – my son Quintin Kucera for inspiring me with your humor, creativity, and joy. To my dad Tom Burnett for teaching me how to perform and work hard, and for instilling in me a love of gardening. To my mom Kathy Burnett, for inspiring me to take risks and follow my heart, and for teaching me how to dance. To my Grandma Schweizer, for instilling a matrilineal entrepreneurial spirit into my mother, aunt, and I. And to my earth, blood, and soul brother Dustin Burnett for being my BFF on this journey of life. And the mother of all mothers, our great Mama Earth.

About The Author

Women's business & leadership coach, circle & retreat facilitator, author, yoga teacher, and seasonal living advocate, Ashley Burnett has created a 20-year strong global entrepreneurial and wellness movement.

She helps entrepreneurs, artists, healers, and creatives buy back hours of their free time, increase their income, become more impactful leaders, and seasonally align their businesses for heightened profitability, sustainability, and joy.

She also leads women's seasonally focused ritual circles and wellness retreats that inspire more meaning, well-being, mindfulness, and magic.

Ashley has facilitated hundreds of classes, workshops, events, and retreats, and has taught thousands of heart-centered change-makers around the globe.

She just migrated back to her hometown hamlet of Quincy, IL on the Mississippi River, after 18 years in the San Francisco Bay Area – along with her husband David and sweet son Quintin.

She's launching her Wellness and Creativity Studio and Retreat Space, *The Gathering Ground* in 2024.

Visit **ashleyburnett.co** to learn more.

Notes

www.ingramcontent.com/pod-product-compliance
Lightning Source LLC
Chambersburg PA
CBHW050732010526
44107CB00010B/816